My Beautiful
Masterpiece

GABRIELLE HAWKINS

Copyright © 2024 Gabrielle Hawkins
All rights reserved
First Edition

PAGE PUBLISHING
Conneaut Lake, PA

First originally published by Page Publishing 2024

ISBN 979-8-89157-820-3 (pbk)
ISBN 979-8-89157-838-8 (digital)

Printed in the United States of America

Darling wanting the same energy as you give is not asking for too much
You deserve to be filled the same way you pour
You deserve happiness
And that boy who swore he loved you but yet used you
To his own advantage never deserved you, my amazing, beautiful girl.

I wish you could feel the way my heart shattered when you left
Without any explanation
No reason why you thought I was not enough for you
I wish you knew how many nights I cried myself to sleep
How many times I looked in the mirror and judged every inch of my body
Judged how my stomach has enough stretch marks to wrap around the world two times
Or how my hair is not long and pretty like the girls in the magazines
How my waist could stretch the length of a football field
I wish you knew how I critique myself now more than ever…

Cutting people off to benefit your mental health
Does not make you selfish
You are supposed to be able to grow and blossom
Without people cutting your beautiful petals off
Or covering you in darkness to where you wilt and wither.

If I got another chance…
I promise to make you my whole world
Motivate you to be the best you can be
Tell you how much I appreciate you every day.
Show you what a real home full of love feels like.
Our memories would dance around the room as the love showers down upon us
I would promise to cherish you and give you my heart wrapped in a box with a bow of compassion and meaning
I will wear your favorite lingerie
And we can make love all night
So if we get another chance I will be sure to overfill your cup with love
Because you deserve the best of me, you deserve the new me.

You do not need to apologize for how you feel
You should be able to process your feelings without judgment
You are supposed to process all of your feelings without being
    criticized
So honey goes through the whole process

I always thought home was a place filled with walls
Windows and floors
But you are my home
You are the reason I breathe
The reason a fire is ignited within my soul
The reason I feel safe from this terrible world
I could never muster up enough words
To tell you just how much I appreciate you
My love

And even if we never speak again
Or our paths never cross
I will forever remember the way
Your lips felt against mine
The way you made me feel whole

Taking a break from everyone is fine
It is okay to take a break from the world
to go to a new place, start fresh, meet new people
IT IS OKAY TO FIND YOUR PEACE.

It is okay if you can't get out of bed today
It's okay if you don't wanna be around anyone or go anywhere
It is okay if you want to turn your phone off and just listen to
    the silence
We all have bad days, so take it one step at a time
No one should judge you on how you process your feelings
Or how you cope with your mental health.

And if the world decided to rip us apart from each other
I would be glad that I even had the opportunity to lay my eyes
    on you
The opportunity to be filled with true love that no one could
    ever take away from me
A love that people crave

It is okay if it takes you longer than others
Life is not meant to be rushed
You will get where you need to be
You'll find who you're meant to be with in due time
Be patient, you are the most amazing person ever
Do not forget that.

It is okay if you are not as hungry today as you were yesterday
Do not let anyone judge you on what you eat or how frequently
    you eat
You are perfect, my lovely.

My darling, you need to understand
Not all men mean what they say so
Be careful and guard that pretty heart of yours
It deserves more than lies and broken promises
You are an amazing person, don't ever forget that.
You deserve the whole world don't settle for less

No calls
No texts
No communication
No problem
They do not deserve your time or attention

What a beautiful flower you are my love
With your petals reaching toward the sun
Toward new beginnings, greater things
More opportunities just take a deep breath
You are doing an amazing job

It is okay to feel like you are failing at everything
That you can't do anything right
Just please remember
That you are doing the best you can
That is all that matters, it is okay
You are amazing, hold your head up
My beautiful sunflower is going to get better.
YOU ARE ENOUGH, YOU ARE LOVED

The moment I laid my eyes on you I knew I had to have you
You looked so perfect to me
Such a pure soul
The way you came into my life
You opened up doors that I had bolted shut
The way you made me feel so loved and full
I couldn't have asked for anyone better
From the late nights we spent laughing in the kitchen
To date nights under the stars
You poured your love into me
And for once I felt so at peace
I felt as though the stars aligned and the moon was pulled down
    for me
You were my prize
My handsome man

My Beautiful Masterpiece

I am careful about who I allow into my life
And who I allow to touch my soul

And when they ask you about me
I hope it makes your throat burn
I hope you can't speak
I hope all the memories come flooding back
And you become very weak
I hope you fall to your knees wishing
Wishing you could have me again
I hope you tremble as my name leaves your tongue

What is it? What's wrong?

I don't think anyone noticed how bad it's becoming

I think too much
I feel too much

I overthink

I'm a mess
But I promise I'm trying

I want to feel you
I want you to ignite a fire within my soul
I want you to pull me close
Wrap me up in a blanket of love
Surround me with beautiful flowers
Float me within the clouds
So I can pull the stars down for you
So I can bring you the sun
For you to feel the sweet warmth of my love
Within your soul

It's 2:00 a.m. and the silence covers me like a blanket
Depression and anxiety are racing in my head
And tonight depression is taking top place
As I drown myself deeper and deeper
In the idea of being alone or forgotten
Why am I like this?
What kind of person am I?
What am I here?
These questions fill my brain
As if I've been given a writing assignment by a teacher
I cover myself in this blanket of thoughts
until sleep is my only option.

You filled my heart with a foundation of broken promises
Spun a web full of lies
In fact you never loved me
You never cared about me at all
You only cared about yourself
I was the take-one-and-pass-it-on card within your deck of cards
But to me you were the sun
The stars within my universe
The one thing I needed more than anything

I never thought in a million years I'd lose you
Never in a thousand lifetimes
Would I picture myself without you by my side
As the laughter fills the room
My love
where did you go
Why don't you stay

He's never coming back
My brain whispered
But he has to
My heart sobbed

I feel like I am drowning
As though I'm at the bottom of the ocean
Weighed down with cinder blocks
Bound with chains
Unable to escape
Unable to speak
Just there
Drowning within my own mind
Within my own feelings
Someone please save me

I want a love
A love that ignites my bones
A love that will never fade
A love that will cause my heart to do backflips
A love that our kids will forever speak of
A love that will follow us until we are old
Unable to speak
A love so pure
A love as sweet as honey and as rich as chocolate

I wish we would have met sooner
Maybe things would have been better
I could have held you longer
Whispered I love you more
Could have held you closer
Begged you to stay
Instead of running away
Could have walked down the aisle
Watching the tears roll down your face
As you said I do
But for now I will dream about it
How our future could have been so different
How possibly, maybe
I wouldn't be crying myself to sleep every night
Wishing I could rewind time
Wishing I could tell you that you are mine

I'm not sorry for the things that I said
And I'm not sorry that you didn't know
How to properly love me
How to protect me
When everything was being thrown at me
I am not sorry for how I chose to express my emotions
I was only a child

And to my younger self
You did not deserve all of the pain
You did not deserve to be embedded with thorns
You did not deserve to feel as though you weren't enough
My beautiful child you were more than enough
You were the whole world
The reason why stars shined so bright
Within the sky
So happy
So free
So full of hope and love

I looked up at the sky
To find the moon was full
Shining so bright
But yet the stars were gone
the rest of the world seemed so dark
And it got me thinking
Thinking about how you are the moon
And I am the stars
Without you I am nothing
Without you I am just existing

I am proud of my heart
It has been through hell
It has been through heartbreak
It has been through grief
It has been filled with loneliness
And washed with false hope
I am proud of my heart because
Even though it has been stomped
Crushed
Trampled on
Shattered into a million pieces
Surprisingly it still works
Surprisingly I am still here
Trying to love
Trying to be happy
Trying to be better

My Beautiful Masterpiece

So thank you
Thank you for filling my life with happiness
Thank you for making me feel
As though the moon and stars
Were made for me
How could I ever muster the words
To tell you just how much I love you
I could sit here and compile a list
But We would be here for an eternity

I find it remarkable that you get up every day
Even if you long to lay in bed
Even if you are drowning in a sea of depression
Even though your heart is aching
And you are washed over with anxiety
I find it remarkable that even though you are
Longing to shut everyone out
You still get up, get dressed, and go about your day

If I had the chance
I would kiss your forehead
As you lay asleep next to me
I would whisper in your ear
How mesmerizing you are to me
How I could stare into your blue eyes all day
If I had the chance I would lasso the sun
So that I could brighten up the hardest of days
I would fold you up and put you in my pocket
So that I would never be without you
If I had the chance
I wouldn't have messed it up this time
There would be no lies
No arguments
Just love

It is okay to heal
It is okay if you
Can not forgive the people
Who hurt you just yet
You are doing a great job

I feel a heavy weight
Crushing my chest
An ache that will never go away
A feeling as though
My heart is shattering
That my life is slowly falling apart
As though no matter what I do
I will still be in the same situation
My heart is heavy
I feel as though
My lungs will collapse at any second

Craving a life I can only dream about
A life full of love
Happiness
A life where we could
Sit on our porch and listen
To the rain fall on the roof
As I feel your hand running through my hair
While the crickets chirp
As I listen to you go on and on about your day

Don't tell me I am too emotional
I am healing
Don't tell me I am failing
I am healing
Don't tell me that the world doesn't revolve around me
I am healing
Don't tell me I ask for too much
I am healing

The smell of your cologne
Fills the air But yet you aren't here
You're nowhere to be found
The sweet notes of bergamot
Sticks to my sheets
As I begin to fall asleep
Fall asleep and dream about
You and me

As I lay in bed
Staring at the ceiling
A familiar smell fills the room
And our memories start to replay in my mind
The biggest smile comes across my face
And I begin to feel my heart race
Oh how I love you
How I love every single inch of you

My trauma follows me
Just like a ghost
Haunting my existence
My trauma shatters me
As though I am a piece of art
Being tossed on the floor
I wish my trauma would go
I wish my trauma was someone I could
Cut off and never see again
I wish my trauma would die
Be buried six feet deep unable
For me to touch again

I'm sorry that I love too hard
I'm sorry I come with trust issues
And worries that could last a lifetime
I'm sorry that I'm damaged from past lovers
Who ripped me to pieces
The same way carnivorous animals
Eat their prey
I'm learning
Please be patient with me

You never asked me how my day was
You didn't even know my favorite color
I don't think you even really cared

But two years was way too long for me to let go
Especially at that age

It made me sick to my stomach
How much I loved you
How I would've died for you
I would've did anything in my power to give you the world
But you, you didn't even care if the clouds parted
and the sun showered down on me

The sad truth is
Even if you deleted me
Blocked my number
Told me I wasn't what you wanted
I would still choose you
I would choose you in every lifetime

While playing with my hair
You told me I was pretty
You told me I was everything you wanted
You told me that I ignited a flame
Within your soul unlike no other
You promised to love and protect me
That everything was gonna be okay
I confided in you
I trusted you
I let you in
And after so long
You changed
You became bitter
You began to treat me
Like the last piece of candy that no one wanted
Like I left a sour taste in your mouth
You began to shower me with bruises
And marks that I never once asked for
You brought in the worst storm I have ever seen
And left me completely and utterly demolished

Remember to breathe my love

For a moment I was happy
Like the clouds parted and allowed
A little bit of sun to find me
For a moment the stars shined so bright
The planets rotated completely
The world felt right again
And I was at peace
Then
Then the waves came crashing into me
Pulling me under
Back into the sea of depression that
I can never seem to escape

Remember you have survived the toughest things, this too shall pass
Breathe it's going to be alright

Take me back to when all I had to worry about
Was taking a nap and what clothes to wear to school
When I was only worried about my socks matching
And if my crush was going to be in class
When I didn't have a care in the world
And I didn't mind if my thighs touched
Or if my hair was a mess
When I was truly happy

Darling I know you are tired
I know your soul is aching for rest
I know your feet are dragging on the floor
I know your heart is slowly shattering
But you have to keep going
You have to keep pushing forward
No matter how much pain it hurts
Don't give up not yet

You've survived the things that should have broken you
The things that would have made anyone else fold
You are strong
You are courageous
Take it easy on yourself

But you weren't just a chapter
You were my whole damn book
But I, I was just a stupid paragraph
Hell maybe just a sentence in yours
I could sit down and write word after word
About you I could draw out
A line of phrases and quotes to
Express my dying love for you
And yet you could only write one little sentence

You are a beautiful tree
With its roots planted firmly into the ground
Branches spread far and wide growing oh so beautifully
With the most amazing flowers I have ever seen
Steadily growing reaching toward the sun

When I hit rock bottom
No hand or rope appeared
And I wondered
If nothing wanted me
Cause I don't even want me
Maybe I am both good and bad

Thoughts raging through my mind
I toss and I turn but yet I lie awake
I wish sleep would cover me like a blanket
That I would go into a deep slumber
I wish for peace, please
Let me sleep

My beautiful masterpiece
You look exactly like me
From your curly hair
To the way you speak
You are the best pieces of me
You are the one thing that I can never lose
You are my creation
Carried within my womb
You are the one thing that saved me
My motivation
My happiness
My never-ending love

Follow your dream they say
But what if my dreams are filled with nightmares
Filled with monsters chasing me in an endless cycle
No matter how fast I run they always pull my feet out from under me
They drag me
Suffocate me
Chain me to a wall of endless thoughts
Throwing their taunting words at me
As though I can dodge every single one of them
As if I am invincible
As if I can conquer the world

When will you have enough?
When will you stop to realize that this isn't how someone is supposed to be treated?
When will you see that there are way better people in the world?
Stop worrying about the people who let you go, the people who threw you to the side like you never even existed. When will you realize that there is so much love in the world, so many new faces you haven't even met yet

And if the universe tears us apart
I will never lose someone the way I love you
I will never be able to look into someone's eyes
And see my whole future with them
Because you are my soulmate
My twin flame
The one I have been waiting for

For once I want someone to be afraid to lose me

How was I
Supposed to know
That you wouldn't be mine
How was I supposed to know
You didn't like the way I parted my hair
Or the way my thighs touched

I am convinced you thought my heart was a pinata
Something you could play with and bash around
Until you got bored
But my heart is not a pinata
It is not filled with candy
It is not meant to be broken
Shattered
Tossed around like it's nothing
I thought you knew that

If I could speak to you one last time
I would tell you that you were enough
It was my fault
I ruined everything
If we could speak one last time
I would scream at the top of my lungs
I LOVE YOU
I loved the way you look at me
I loved the way my name rolled off your tongue
I absolutely love the way your face is covered in freckles
I loved the way you smile as I look at you
I loved the way you held me when I felt like the world was
      falling apart
If I could speak to you one last time
I would tell you
Over and over again I love you

Through all the darkness
All the pain I've felt within my bones
All of the nights I cried myself to sleep
Through all of the bad things life has thrown at me
You found your way to me
You brought back the happiness
You brought back the life I've so ever dreamed about

I want flowers on a random Tuesday
I want long walks on the beach
While we listen to the waves crashing
And I feel the sand beneath our feet
I want laughter to echo off the walls within our home
I want horror movies and pizza
I want cuddles on the couch even though we will both pass out
I want everything
With you

My mind is an ocean
With waves constantly crashing all around me
With a current so strong that I cannot seem to escape
No matter how fast I swim no matter how much I try
I still seem to get ripped under
I can feel the water invading my lungs
Filling every space in my body
Until I become heavy
Weighed down with sadness
Longing for someone to pull me out

Mind wants rest
Body wants sleep

I love you he whispered
As if I knew what those three words meant
So I mumbled why
Why do you love me
To which he replied
Because, Because you make my days bearable
You make my heart flutter and my hands shake when I'm around you
Because you are the one thing I can't live without
But that's silly how can one man love me that much
As if I am a goddess for him to worship
As if I am the only reason he's breathing

Don't fucking tell me I could do better
When he was my whole heart
He was my forever

That damn mirror
I hate that damn mirror
It makes me feel as though I am not enough
As though I am fat and ugly
That mirror makes me hate every inch of my body
That mirror makes me wanna jump out of my own school
That damn mirror makes me wonder if I will ever be
Pretty enough for anyone to love
Wondering if I will ever be able to look at myself
And see the beautiful person I am

I don't think you're hard to love
I think you are the easiest person to love
Loving you has been the easiest thing I've ever done
It's like my purpose is to love you completely
My heart is finally complete
I look at you and I feel peace
I look at you and I feel
an unconditional love
I promise it's not hard to love you
It is impossible for me not to

I feel a blanket of darkness covering me
I shouldn't feel this way
I should be happy
Laughing
Enjoying life
But something
Something keeps pulling me
Back into this pit of darkness that
I can never seem to escape
No matter how fast I run
I cannot escape it

Be patient with me
I am healing from things I don't care to talk about
Things I would never wish upon anyone
Things I thought only existed in my nightmares
Things I have not yet begun to process
Things I wish I could forget about
Be patient with me
Though my anger
My Depression
My quietness
I am stuck in the maze in my mind trying to escape
But no matter how I try I always come to a dead end
So please be patient with me
I am healing

I am not the type of girl that guys fall in love with
I am the type of girl guys will use and abuse
Use to keep themselves busy until
The girl they actually want comes along
And I know why
I am too nice
I long to please everyone
I am an old soul with an even older heart
I chose to see the good in people
I let things slide
I am gullible
I allow people to break me down
I am too easy
I am too trusting

I wish I was one of the girls on the magazine covers with
Flawless skin
Thigh gaps
Long blonde hair
A flat stomach
The type of girls guys actually want
The type of girl that gets invited everywhere
I wish I was one of the girls that didn't have to worry about
Their weight or what they eat for dinner
I wish I was a girl who could be happy inside her own skin
Someone who did not get bombarded with insults
Someone who could wake up every morning and feel beautiful

I would ask why
Why would you come into my life
Promise me everything
Promise me endless love
A love that I constantly crave
Maybe I am stupid for thinking
That someone could actually love me
Someone could actually deal with all of my trauma
My anxiety, depression
All the demons that lie in my head
Constantly pushing to the surface
I am tired of broken promises and constant lies
I wake up throughout the night constantly
Unable to be settled

I grew up in a house where
Arguments bounced off the walls like
Music in a cathedral
Where I'm sorry was absent
Where I-love-yous were barely spoken
Where the way I felt about myself didn't matter
I grew up in a home where
I had to pretend I was okay
I had to act like my mental health was in perfect check
And I wasn't crying myself to sleep every night
Wishing things were different
I grew up in a home where hugs were never given
And the words you're doing amazing were never spoken

It's funny
How you wanted me first
And after making me feel
Like I was the only girl on
This whole planet
You left
Without saying a word
Without any explanation
Leaving me craving someone
I could never have again

Those blue eyes
They get me every time
They make me feel as though
Heaven created you just for me
That damn smile
I could stare at it every morning as I opened my eyes
That curly hair
I would never get tired of having my fingers intertwined in it
My love
My sweet love
My handsome man
My other half
No amount of words could express my love and gratitude for you
No gesture could even come close
You are worth more than any amount of words or poems I could ever write

My darling
It is okay to still be broken over someone
Who meant everything to you
You are slowly learning how to be yourself again
It is okay to cry into your pillow wishing the world
Would be quiet
It is okay to feel
To accept that things are over
It is okay to scream from the top of your lungs
Let it out my dear sweet child

Never let him put his hands on you and treat you as though
You are not his whole world
You deserve roses on a Tuesday
Random coffee dates
You deserve to be completely loved
Valued as a whole person
You deserve to be shown
What real love is
Not to be used for your body or money
You are not a piece of meat
You are a piece of artwork
It's okay to wait for the right person
Someone to wrap you in happiness
So hold your head up all the tears shall pass
All the lonely nights crying yourself to sleep will come to an end
And you will find a man who will worship the ground you walk
    on

I don't think I'll ever be able to love
Not like the way I loved you
You are the only person I want to love like this
I promise
I will hold onto the idea of us
Until the last breath leaves my lungs

I've hated the person I've become
So cold, so numb
As though my heart is an iceberg rock-hard
Frozen, dead in its tracks
As though I am unable to feel anything again
I hate that I can't sympathize with anyone
I can't bother to show my gratitude for anything let alone anyone
When did I become so distant
So eager to cut everyone off and never speak again
Turn on survival mode and move in silence
The thought of it all is deadly
When did I become this monster of a person
Unable to open up to anyone
Unable to speak my truth and accept the things I can't control.

I would like to think that somewhere in the universe
You're thinking about me
Thinking about all the memories
I would like to think that this meeting was fate
And that even though we can't be together right now
That one day we will find our way back to each other
But what I don't understand is how could you promise me
The whole world the moon and the stars and then rip it all away
How could you take my happiness and throw it in the trash
Like it never meant anything to you I should hate you
But yet I still love you

You have literally destroyed
Every inch of me
Bone to bone
Vein to vein

Guys like skinny girls
The mirror whispers to me
As I stared at my naked body
Counting every crevice and fat roll on my body
Wondering if I will ever be able to feel beautiful in my own skin
Your hair isn't long enough
Your shoulders are too wide
You will never find someone to love you
It echoes in my mind It plays on repeat
Like a song I cannot get out of my head
Trapped in my own personal hell
Population me

I can't admit that it's over between us
That I will no longer get to touch your face
Or feel your lips pressed against mine
That I will no longer be able to call you
At 3:00 a.m. when the world feels like it is falling apart
And I'm getting ripped into shreds
I will no longer be able to look at your photo and say this is my forever
I will never be able to feel your hand run through my hair or down my spine
But god I wanted you to be my last
I wanted you to be the person I ran to when all felt lost
But at last my heart is shattered and my lungs are exhausted
From all the nights I cried myself to sleep

If we could speak one last time
I would tell you that you were enough
It was my fault
I ruined everything
If we could speak one last time
I would scream at the top of my lungs
I LOVE YOU
I loved the way you look at me
I loved the way my name rolled off your tongue
I absolutely love the way your face is covered in freckles
I loved the way you smile as I look at you
I loved the way you held me when I felt like the whole world
    was falling apart
If I could speak to you one last time
I would tell you over and over again
I love you

I wish I could tell whoever came up with I love you
That those three little words have the most power in the entire
    world
Those three little words can destroy you
Because to be told I love you without true meaning
Can break your fucking heart
I wish I could give a big fuck you
To whoever came up with those three little words

I never believed in soul mates
But I swear the moment
I laid my eyes on you
My soul was at peace
My heart full
Happiness consumed me

I'm sorry that the people who were supposed to make you feel safe
Filled you with trauma and caused you so much pain
That they made you feel as though your existence had no meaning
That everything you have ever done was wrong
I'm sorry that you had to go through everything on your own
Unable to speak about your feelings
Unable to handle your depression and anxiety
I'm sorry you are left to heal from the things you can't bear to talk about
You deserve nothing but love
you deserve to believe that the world isn't so cold

Thank you
For putting up with me on my bad days
For reminding me that I am capable of being loved
For reminding me what I'm worth
Thank you
For shining light into my life
For filling my heart with love

I am a ghost
Well not really
I am here but I'm not here
I don't feel anything
I lack motivation
I don't wanna go anywhere
I don't look forward to the morning
All of my demons are playing poker with each other
While I suit up to fight the battle on my own

"I'm scared," she whispered.

"Of what?" he replied.

"Scared that you will wake up one day and realize you no longer want me.
That I will become a distant memory to you, a stranger.
That you will find better and I will end up utterly alone.
Because everyone leaves."

"Why are you so quiet?" she asks
As though I can formulate any kind of answer
"I'm tired," I reply
But I'm not really tired
I'm just filled with complete and utter silence
I'm numb
I am fighting to keep myself alive
But no one needs to know
No one needs to be bombarded by the demons I hold inside

Who do I run to
When the person I need the most
Is nowhere to be found
When my safe place is shattered
Demolished
In ruins
And I cannot fix it by myself

Ever since you left
I have been mad at the world
Filled with such anger that I cannot seem to extinguish
Such an empty hole I cannot seem to fill
Why?
Why did you have to get taken away
Without any reason or explanation
I don't think I'll ever feel the same again

I'm sorry that I question your love
I'm sorry that I put myself down
And tell you that you deserve better
I'm sorry that you have to deal with all my damage
I love you
I promise
I am trying my best

Breathe in everything is okay
Take it day by day
Moment by moment
Until you feel okay again
Everything will work out
The world will feel whole again
You are an amazing person
Keep going

Today I learned that It only takes seven to ten years for our cells to regenerate
So only two to five years for me to have a body you never touched
A body you never abused
A body where your handprints were never left
A body with a clean slate
A body with fresh skin glowing with health
Instead of a body holding onto years of trauma

One step at a time
I am taking it one step at a time
Slowly making my way through
This crazy thing called life

I watched in silence
As your love for me
Drained from your body

I wish we were strangers
That I never laid my eyes on you
I did not deserve the pain
Nor abuse you subjected me to
I did not deserve the manipulation
Or the marks you left on my skin
Or the anxiety that now fills my bones

All I did was try to love you the best I could
And all you did is make it worse

We may not be talking right now
But I remember the nights we stayed up
Laughing

I did not ask
For you to destroy me
To break every
Single wall within me
To shatter my heart
And puncture my lungs
I didn't ask to be
Used to your advantage
All I wanted was love

I lie awake at night
Wondering if you'll
Get tired of me
Just like everyone else

How could you declare your love for me
Tell me that I ignite a fire within
Your soul
Show me your true self
Just to turn around and
Shatter my heart

Why are you acting so weird?

You have no idea how much pain I'm in

The weather is getting colder
And the sadness is creeping back in
My bed feels so comfortable
I'm constantly trying to fill a gaping hole
In my chest
Because nowhere feels like home

"I love you"

"Yet you make me feel like I am nothing"

I replay that night in my head
Over and over again on repeat
How you forced your hands on my body
How you took something that wasn't yours
How could you treat me as though
I was a piece of meat
For you to use whenever you felt like it
My trust is gone
My body is numb

I screamed from the top of my lungs
Trying to explain how I feel
And to validate my feelings
But no one listened

Constantly wondering how the days had gotten away from me
How my whole childhood flashed before my eyes
And I can't remember any of it

I say that all bodies are beautiful
But I refuse to look at mine
I refuse to think I'm pretty

Flashes of memories dance in my head
Of random things I seemed to forget
Memories I buried deep down
Within my soul
For these memories leave a
Disgusting taste in my mouth
A taste I can never seem to get rid of

I have nothing left to give
I am an empty shell

I told you
All my worst fears
Everything I went through
And yet you used it against me
Used it to manipulate me
Into staying
How dare you

You keep calling
Yet I don't answer
You do not deserve
My time nor energy

I do not have any more
Love to give
I am drained
I am tired of giving my energy to
People who don't deserve it

My demons call me
In the middle of the night
Whispering
Rude things to me
Filling my head with nonsense
All of these words they
Engrave in my head
When will it stop

It hurts
It hurts so much
But I'll keep it to myself
So I don't annoy anyone with my problems

I crave you
I crave holding you
Until the sun comes up
Having you whisper
I love you
As I lay on your chest

When I die
Don't cry I was already dead
I just fell asleep

This is the type of sadness
That makes me feel as though
The world is on fire and
I cannot extinguish it
My bucket of water
Is of no help
I am fucked

When
When did everything go wrong
You once loved me
You once dreamed about a life with me
About us dancing around the living room
We were so in love
We were destined to be
But now you're someone I do not recognize
You've changed
Became cold, bitter

You invade my dreams
Tiptoeing around reminding me
That you aren't mine to love anymore
But god the memories flood back
At least in my dreams I can enjoy you
One last time

I was in the darkness for so long
But you, you brought back the light
That I was so desperately needing
You brought back the love that I
Forgot the taste of
You filled me with the warmest feeling
I love you so much

Three a.m. and my mind is racing
Stuck replaying every bad memory
Every pain I have ever encountered
Feeling as though I am on a merry-go-round
Going in repeated circles
Unable to escape my thoughts

When the world feels so lonely
I will be here to
Hold your hand through everything

I would wait months
I would wait years
I will wait however long it takes
For us to find ourselves
Because the moment I met you
I knew we were meant for each other

You are the reason I
Wake up with a smile on my face
The reason I believe in love again
You are my soulmate

We may be young but
I want us to last a lifetime

People leave
People change
But you will always
Have me no matter what

Dance with me at 2:00 a.m.
Love me at my worst
Support me at my best

I refuse to believe that every bad thing happens for no reason
We are meant to grow
We are meant to become stronger from the pain we endure
We are resilient

About the Author

Gabrielle Hawkins grew up in the small town of Molino, Florida, and has been expressing herself through writing since high school. Writing had always been her solace, a way to escape the chaos of life and find peace within the pages of her own creation. It was during a period of personal struggle that she found solace in books, and they became her guiding light. Inspired by this transformative experience, she embarked on a journey to write a book that would help others navigate their own challenges. Gabrielle is currently going to college to further her career within the healthcare field so that she may continue to help people.

Printed in the USA
CPSIA information can be obtained
at www.ICGtesting.com
LVHW041057130624
783006LV00003B/347